To:

_____ Pat _____

Love From:

_____ Ruth + Steven _____

Date:

_____ Dec 2001 _____

For when we bring some pleasure
To another human heart,
We have followed in His footsteps
And we've had a little part

– *Helen Steiner Rice* –

PEARLS OF
Remembrance

HELEN STEINER RICE

Christian Art Gifts

Pearls of remembrance contains excerpts from
A book of blessings, first published by Fleming
H. Revell, a division of Baker Book House Company,
PO Box 6287, Grand Rapids, MI 49516-6287

© 1995 by Virginia J. Ruehlmann and
The Helen Steiner Rice Foundation
Compiled by Virginia J. Ruehlmann

First edition published in South Africa by Christian Art Publishers
PO Box 1599, Vereeniging, 1930
© 1996

Second edition © 2000 by Christian Art Gifts

Cover designed by Christian Art Gifts

Scripture quotations marked RSV are taken from
the Revised Standard Version of the Bible, copyright
1946, 1952, 1971, 1973 by the Division of
Christian Education of the National Council of the
Churches of Christ in the United States of America.

Scripture verses marked NIV are taken from the *Holy Bible*,
New International Version®. NIV®. Copyright © 1973,
1978, 1984 by International Bible Society. Used by
permission of Zondervan Publishing House. All rights reserved.

Scripture selections from the New American Bible (NAB),
copyright © 1970 by the Confraternity of Christian Doctrine,
Washington D.C., are used with permission. All rights reserved.

Printed and bound in Hong Kong

ISBN 1-86852-607-0

00 01 02 03 04 05 06 07 08 09 - 10 9 8 7 6 5 4 3 2 1

Contents

The Helen Steiner Rice Foundation

The Helen Steiner Rice Foundation

Whatever the celebration, whatever the day, whatever the event, whatever the occasion, Helen Steiner Rice possessed the ability to express the appropriate feeling for that particular moment in time.

A happening became happier, a sentiment more sentimental, memory more memorable because of her deep sensitivity to put into understandable language the emotion being experienced. Her positive attitude, her concern for others, and her love of God are identifiable threads woven into her life, her work ... and even her death.

Prior to Mrs. Rice's passing, she established the *Helen Steiner Rice Foundation*, a nonprofit corporation whose purpose is to award grants to worthy charitable programs that assist the elderly and the needy.

Royalties from the sale of this book will add to the financial capabilities of the *Helen Steiner Rice Foundation*. Because of limited resources, the foundation presently limits grants to qualified charitable programs in Lorain, Ohio, where Helen Steiner Rice was born, and Greater Cincinnati, Ohio, where Mrs. Rice lived and worked most of her life. Hopefully, in the near future, resources will be of sufficient size that broader areas can be considered for the awarding of grants.

Because of her foresight, caring, and deep conviction of sharing, Helen Steiner Rice continues to touch a countless number of lives through grants and through her inspirational poetry.

Virginia J. Reuhlmann, Administrator
The Helen Steiner Rice Foundation
Suite 2100, Atrium Two
221 E. Fourth Street
Cincinatti, Ohio 45201

Introduction

Wishing God's sweet blessings
Not in droplets but a shower,
To fall on you throughout the day
And brighten every hour.

A pilgrimage to the Holy Land increases one's faith, inspirations, and amazement. Visiting Capernaum and the Sea of Galilee sparks an incredible realization that the visitor is perhaps walking the same path that Jesus traveled when He delivered the Sermon on the Mount. His words in that sermon startled the crowd and challenged the basic attitudes and values of that day – and the present!

Envision Jesus climbing the mountainside with the crowd following, finding a level spot, and sitting down to teach, as was the custom then for rabbis. The listeners were amazed at His message.

The Beatitudes promised that many blessings are available when we live our individual lives in a fashion that is pleasing to God and when we concentrate on important Christian values rather than unimportant worldly aspects.

If Jesus were to deliver His Sermon on the Mount today, our secular world would again be startled. The lessons in the Beatitudes are equally important and timely in the here and now as in the day when spoken originally by Jesus. His principles stressed a lifestyle of agape love, charity, forgiveness, humility, trust and a dependence upon God rather than the worldly goals of wealth, pleasure, and self-justification.

Helen Steiner Rice endeavored to live by the philosophy espoused by Jesus. Her poetry vividly, effectively, and inspirationally expresses the same spiritual concepts and values that are inherent in the message of the Beatitudes.

May *A Book of Blessings* be a blessing in your life and, by your example and actions, may your life be a blessing to others. Permit God's love to flow through you.

May God's choicest blessings be yours.

– *Virginia J. Reuhlmann* –

BLESSINGS IN TIMES OF TRIAL

Blessed are those who mourn,
for they will be comforted.

 Matthew 5:4 NIV

Count your gains and not your losses

As we travel down life's busy road
Complaining of our heavy load,
We often think God's been unfair
And gave us much more than our share
Of daily little irritations
And disappointing tribulations.

We're discontented with our lot
And all the bad breaks that we got.
We count our losses not our gain,
And remember only tears and pain.
The good things we forget completely –
When God looked down and blessed us
    sweetly.

Our troubles fill our every thought –
We dwell upon the goals we sought
And, wrapped up in our own despair,
We have no time to see or share
Another's load that far outweighs
Our little problems and dismays.

And so we walk with heads held low,
And little do we guess or know
That someone near us on life's street
Is burdened deeply with defeat,
And if we'd but forget our care
And stop in sympathy to share
The burden that our brother carried,
Our minds and hearts would be less harried
And we would feel our load was small –
In fact, we carried no load at all.

*When you reap your harvest in your field, and
have forgotten a sheaf in the field, you shall not
go back to get it; it shall be for the sojourner, the
fatherless, and the widow; that the Lord your
God may bless you in all the work of your hands.*

• Deuteronomy 24:19 RSV •

I said a special prayer for you

I said a birthday prayer for you
    and I asked the Lord above
To keep you safely in His care
    and enfold you in His love.
I did not ask for fortune,
    for riches or for fame –
I only asked for blessings
    in the Savior's holy name
Blessings to surround you
    in times of trial and stress,
And inner joy to fill your heart
    with peace and happiness.

*May the Lord give strength
to his people! May the Lord
bless his people with peace!*

Psalm 29:11 RSV

The blessing
of sharing

Only what we give away
Enriches us from day to day,
For not in getting but in giving
Is found the lasting joy of living,
For no one ever had a part
In sharing treasures of the heart
Who did not feel the impact of
The magic mystery of God's love.
Love alone can make us kind
And give us joy and peace of mind,
So live with joy unselfishly
And you'll be blessed abundantly.

Blessed are they who maintain justice,
who constantly do what is right.

Psalm 106:3 NIV

A time of renewal

No one likes to be sick
   and yet we know
It takes sunshine and rain
   to make flowers grow ...
And if we never were sick
   and we never felt pain,
We'd be like a desert
   without any rain ...
And who wants a life
   that is barren and dry,
With never a cloud
   to darken the sky?
For continuous sun
   goes unrecognized
Like the blessings God sends,
   which are often disguised,
For sometimes a sickness
   that seems so distressing
Is a time of renewal
   and spiritual blessing.

The king will say to those on his right:
"Come, you have my Father's blessing!"

❧ Matthew 25:34 NAB ☙

No room for blessings

Refuse to be discouraged –
   refuse to be distressed,
For when we are despondent,
   our lives cannot be blessed.
Doubt and fear and worry
   close the door to faith and prayer,
And there's no room for blessings
   when we're lost in deep despair.
So remember when you're troubled
   with uncertainty and doubt,
It is best to tell our Father
   what our fear is all about.
For unless we seek His guidance
   when troubled times arise,
We are bound to make decisions
   that are twisted and unwise.
But when we view our problems
   through the eyes of God above,
Misfortunes turn to blessings
   and hatred turns to love.

Blessed by God, because he
has not rejected my prayer or
removed his steadfast love from me!

Psalm 66:20 RSV

17

The blessings of patience and comfort

Realizing my helplessness,
I'm asking God if He will bless
The thoughts you think and all you do
So these dark hours you're passing through
Will lose their grave anxiety
And only deep tranquillity
Will fill your mind and help impart
New strength and courage to your heart.

So take the Savior's loving hand
And do not try to understand –
Just let Him lead you where He will,
Through pastures green and waters still,
And though the way ahead seems steep,
Be not afraid for He will keep
Tender watch through night and day,
And He will hear each prayer you pray.

So place yourself in His loving care
And He will gladly help you bear
Whatever lies ahead of you

For there is nothing God can't do ...
So I commend you into God's care,
And each day I will say a prayer
That you will feel His presence near
To help dissolve your every fear.

Blessed are all those who wait for him.

&ve; Isaiah 30:18 RSV &ve;

OPEN YOUR HEART TO BLESSINGS

Blessed are the meek, for they will inherit the earth.

❧ Matthew 5:5 NIV ❧

My prayer

Bless me, heavenly Father –
   forgive my erring ways.
Grant me strength to serve Thee,
   put purpose in my days.
Give me understanding,
   enough to make me kind,
So I may judge all people
   with my heart and not my mind.
Teach me to be patient
   in everything I do,
Content to trust Your wisdom
   and to follow after You.
Help me when I falter
   and hear me when I pray,
And receive me in Thy kingdom
   to dwell with Thee someday.

O Lord Almighty, blessed
is the man who trusts in you.

Psalm 84:12 NIV

Blessed
little memories

Tender little memories
   of little things we've done
Make the very darkest day
   a bright and happy one.
Tender little memories
   of some word or deed
Give us strength and courage
   when we are in need.
Blessed little memories
   help us bear the cross
And soften all the bitterness
   of failure and of loss.
Priceless little memories
   are treasures you can't buy,
And oh, how poor the world is
   compared to you and I.

*Blessed is he who comes in
the name of the Lord. From the
house of the Lord we bless you.*

Psalm 118:29 NIV

God's Keeping

To be in God's keeping
   is surely a blessing,
For, though life is often
   dark and distressing,
No day is too dark
   and no burden too great
That God in His love
   cannot penetrate ...
And to know and believe
   without question or doubt
That no matter what happens
   God is there to help out
Is to hold in your hand
   the golden key
To peace and joy
   and serenity.

Bless the Lord, O my soul! O Lord
my God, thou art very great!

Psalm 104:1 RSV

Is the cross you wear too heavy to bear?

Complainingly I told myself
    this cross was too heavy to wear,
And I wondered discontentedly
    why God gave it to me to bear.
I looked with envy at others
    whose crosses seemed lighter than mine
And wished that I could change my cross
    for one of a lighter design.

Then in a dream I beheld the cross
    I impulsively wanted to wear –
It was fashioned of pearls and diamonds
    and gems that are precious and rare,
And when I hung it around my neck,
    the weight of the jewels and the gold
Was much too heavy and cumbersome
    for my small, slender neck to hold.

So I tossed it aside, and before my eyes
    was a cross of rose-red flowers,
And I said with delight as I put it on,

"This cross I can wear for hours."
For it was so dainty and fragile,
    so lovely and light and thin,
But I had forgotten about the thorns
    that started to pierce my skin.

Then in a dream I saw my cross –
    rugged and old and plain –
The clumsy old cross I had looked upon
    with discontented disdain,
And at last I knew that God had made
    this special cross for me,
For God in His great wisdom
    knew what I before could not see –
That often the loveliest crosses
    are the heaviest crosses to bear,
For only God is wise enough
    to choose the cross each can wear.

So never complain about your cross,
    for your cross has been blessed –
God made it just for you to wear
    and remember, God knows best.

This blessing has fallen to me,
that I have kept thy precepts.

* Psalm 119:56 RSV *

Look on the
sunny side

જં   ✑

There are always two sides –
    the good and the bad,
The dark and the light,
    the sad and the glad –
But in looking back over
    the good and the bad,
We're aware of the number
    of good things we've had,
And in counting our blessings,
    we find when we're through
We've no reason at all
    to complain or be blue.
So thank God for good things
    He's already done,
And be grateful to Him
    for the battles you've won,
And know that the same God
    who helped you before
Is ready and willing
    to help once more.
Then with faith in your heart,
    reach out for God's hand
And accept what He sends,

though you can't understand …
For our Father in heaven
   always knows what is best,
And if you trust His wisdom,
   your life will be blessed …
For always remember that
   whatever betide you,
You are never alone,
   for God is beside you.

Open the door
to blessings

Father, make us kind and wise
So we may always recognize
The blessings that are ours to take,
The friendships that are ours to make,
If we but open our heart's door wide
To let the sunshine of love inside.

*Sing to the Lord, bless his name; tell
of his salvation from day to day.*

Psalm 96:2 RSV

The autumn of life

What a wonderful time is life's autumn,
   when the leaves of the trees are all gold,
When God fills each day as He sends it
   with memories, priceless and old.
What a treasure-house filled with rare jewels
   are the blessings of year upon year,
When life has been lived as you've lived it
   in a home where God's presence is near ...
May the deep meaning surrounding this day,
   like the paintbrush of God up above,
Touch your life with wonderful blessings
   and fill your heart brimful with His love.

Amen! Blessings and glory and
wisdom and thanksgiving and honor
and power and might be to our
God for ever and ever! Amen.

Revelation 7:12 RSV

SHOWERS
OF
BLESSINGS

*Blessed are the merciful, for
they will be shown mercy.*

 Matthew 5:7 NIV

Showers
of blessings

Each day there are showers of blessings
  sent from the Father above,
For God is a great, lavish giver,
  and there is no end to His love ...
And His grace is more than sufficient,
  His mercy is boundless and deep,
And His infinite blessings are countless –
  and all this we're given to keep
If we but seek God and find Him
  and ask for a bounteous measure
Of this wholly immeasurable offering
  from God's inexhaustible treasure ...
For no matter how big man's dreams are,
  God's blessings are infinitely more,
For always God's giving is greater
  than what man is asking for.

I will send down showers in season;
there will be showers of blessings.

෨ Ezekiel 34:26 NIV ෨

You too must weep

Let me not live a life that's free
From the things that draw me close to Thee,
For how can I ever hope to heal
The wounds of others I do no feel!
If my eyes are dry and I never weep,
How do I know when the hurt is deep!
If my heart is cold and it never bleeds,
How can I tell what my brother needs!
For when ears are deaf to the beggar's plea
And we close our eyes and refuse to see
And we steel our hearts and harden our minds
And we count it a weakness whenever we're
    kind,
We are no longer following the Father's way
Or seeking His guidance from day to day.

For, without crosses to carry and burdens to bear,
We dance through a life that is frothy and fair,
And, chasing the rainbow, we have no desire
For roads that are rough and realms that are
    higher.
So spare me no heartache or sorrow, dear Lord,
For the heart that hurts reaps the richest reward,
And God blesses the heart that is broken with
    sorrow

As He opens the door to a brighter tomorrow.
For only through tears can we recognize
The suffering that lies in another's eyes.

Yet our God turned
the curse into a blessing.

❦ Nehemiah 13:2 RSV ❧

Thank You, God for everything

Thank You, God, for everything –
    the big things and the small –
For every good gift comes from God,
    the Giver of them all,
And all too often we accept
    without any thanks or praise
The gifts God sends as blessings
    each day in many ways.

First, thank You for the little things
    that often come our way –
The things we take for granted
    and don't mention when we pray –

The unexpected courtesy,
    the thoughtful, kindly deed,
A hand reached out to help us
    in the time of sudden need.

Oh, make us more aware, dear God,
    of little daily graces
That come to us with sweet surprise
    from never-dreamed-of places.
Then thank You for the miracles
    we are much too blind to see,
And give us new awareness
    of our many gifts from Thee ...
And help us to remember
    that the key to life and living
Is to make each prayer a prayer of thanks
    and every day Thanksgiving.

The Lord will command the blessing upon
you in your barns, and in all that you
undertake; and he will bless you in the
land which the Lord your God gives you.

এ Deuteronomy 28:8 RSV ক্ষ

God so loved the world

Our Father up in heaven,
  long, long years ago,
Looked down in His great mercy
  upon the earth below
And saw that folks were lonely
  and lost in deep despair,
And so He said, "I'll send My Son
  to walk among them there
So they can hear Him speaking
  and feel His nearness, too,
And see the many miracles
  that faith alone can do,
For I know it will be easier
  to believe and understand
If man can see and talk to Him
  and touch His healing hand."

So whenever we have troubles
  and we're overcome by cares,
We can take it all to Jesus,
  for He understands our prayers.
For He too lived and suffered
  in a world much like our own,

And no man can know the sorrow
     that Jesus Christ has known.

And whatever we endure on earth
     is so very, very small
When compared to God's beloved Son
     who was sent to save us all.
And the blessed reassurance
     that He lived much as we do
Is a source of strength and comfort,
     and it gives us courage, too.

Blessed are all who fear
the Lord, who walk in his ways.

❧ Psalm 128:1 NIV ☙

A thankful heart

Take nothing for granted,
    for whenever you do,
The joy of enjoying
    is lessened for you.
For we rob our own lives
    much more than we know
When we fail to respond
    or in any way show
Our thanks for the blessings
    that daily are ours –
The warmth of the sun,
    the fragrance of flowers,
The beauty of twilight,
    the freshness of dawn,
The coolness of dew
    on a green velvet lawn,
The kind little deeds
    so thoughtfully done,
The favors of friends
    and the love that someone
Unselfishly gives us
    in a myriad of ways,
Expecting no payment
    and no words of praise.
Oh, great is our loss

when we no longer find
A thankful response
to things of this kind,
For the joy of enjoying
and the fullness of living
Are found in the heart
that is filled with thanksgiving.

For seven days you shall keep the
feast to the Lord your God at the
place which the Lord will choose;
because the Lord your God will
bless you in all your produce and
in all the work of your hands, so
that you will be altogether joyful.

❧ Deuteronomy 16:15 RSV ❦

Blessings
devised by God

God speaks to us in many ways,
Altering our lives, our plans and days,
And His blessings come in many guises
That He alone in love devises,
And sorrow, which we dread so much,
Can bring a very healing touch ...
For when we fail to heed His voice
We leave the Lord no other choice
Except to use a firm, stern hand
 To make us know He's in command ...

For on the wings of loss and pain,
The peace we often sought in vain
Will come to us with sweet surprise,
For God is merciful and wise ...
And through dark hours of tribulation
God gives us time for meditation,
And nothing can be counted loss
Which teaches us to bear our cross.

Every day I will bless thee, and
praise thy name for ever and ever.

❧ Psalm 145:2 RSV ❧

Unfailing Blessings

*Blessed are the
peacemakers, for they
will be called sons of God.*

❧ Matthew 5:9 NIV ❧

The first thing every morning and the last thing every night

Were you too busy this morning
  to quietly stop and pray?
Did you hurry and drink your coffee
  then frantically rush away,
Consoling yourself by saying –
  God will always be there
Waiting to hear my petitions,
  ready to answer each prayer!

It's true that the great, generous Savior
  forgives our transgressions each day
And patiently waits for lost sheep
  who constantly seem to stray,
But moments of prayer once omitted
  in the busy rush of the day
Can never again be recaptured,
  for they silently slip away.

Strength is gained in the morning
 to endure the trials of the day
When we visit with God in person
 in a quiet and unhurried way,
For only through prayer that's unhurried
 can the needs of the day be met
And only in prayers said at evening
 can we sleep without fears or regret.

For all of our errors and failures
 that we made in the course of the day
Are freely forgiven at nighttime
 when we kneel down and earnestly pray,
So seek the Lord in the morning
 and never forget Him at night,
For prayer is an unfailing blessing
 that makes every burden seem light.

*May God be gracious to us and bless
us and make his face to shine upon us.*

∾ Psalm 67:1 RSV ∾

God gave
man the earth

"The earth is the Lord's, and thefullness
thereof ... "
He gave it to man as a gift of His love
So all men might live as He hoped they would,
Sharing together all things that were good,
But man only destroyed the good earth of God.
He polluted the air and ravished the soil,
He cut down the forests with ruthless disdain,
And the earth's natural beauty he perverted
    for gain.
And now in an age filled with violent dissent,
Man finds he's imprisoned in his own discontent.
He has taken the earth that God placed in his
    care
And built his own hell without being aware
That the future we face was fashioned by man,
Who in ignorance resisted God's beautiful plan,
And what God created to be paradise
Became by man's lust and perversion and vice
A cauldron of chaos in a fog of pollution
To which man can find no cure or solution.
How far man will go to complete his destruction
Is beyond a computer's robot deduction.

For land which has drunk the rain that
often falls upon it, and brings forth
vegetation useful to those for whose sake it is
cultivated, receives a blessing from God.

∾ Hebrews 6:7 RSV ∾

Counting the blessings

Nothing would make me happier
  or please me any better
Than to write you my thanks
  in a long, friendly letter,
For being remembered
  at the holiday season
By someone like you
  gave my heart ample reason
To count all my blessings,
  and your friendship is one –
For without fans and friends,
  all the writing I've done
Would lose all its meaning
  its warmth and sincereness
For how could I write
  without feeling a nearness
To all the dear people
  who interpret each line
With their own love and kindness,
  which become part of mine,
So, more than you know,
  I thank God above
For fans, friends, and family
  and their gifts of love.

*You shall give to him freely, and
your heart shall not be grudging when
you give to him; because for this the
Lord your God will bless you in all
your work and in all that you undertake.*

∂ Deuteronomy 15:10 RSV ⌒

There is a reason for everything

Our Father knows what's best for us,
    so why should we complain?
We always want the sunshine
    but He knows there must be rain.
We love the sound of laughter
    and the merriment of cheer,
But our hearts would lose their tenderness
    if we never shed a tear.

Our Father tests us often
    with suffering and with sorrow.
He tests us not to punish us
    but help us meet tomorrow,
For growing trees are strengthened
    when they withstand the storm,
And the sharp cut of a chisel
    gives the marble grace and form.

God never hurts us needlessly
    and He never wastes our pain,
For every loss He sends to us
    is followed by rich gain,
And when we count the blessings

that God has so freely sent,
We will find no cause for murmuring
and no time to lament.

For our Father loves His children
and to Him all things are plain,
He never sends us pleasure
when the soul's deep need is pain.
So whenever we are troubled and
when everything goes wrong,
It is just God working in us
to make our spirits strong.

*Blessed is the nation whose
God is the Lord, the people
he chose for his inheritance.*

∾ Psalm 33:12 NIV ∾